Zanzibar and his Zany Crew of Sentence Constructors

Welcome to English!

We are glad that you are here.

Please, come and meet

Zanzibar

and his

Zany Crew of Sentence Constructors!

We are waiting for you . . . .

Please turn the page

Zanzibar and his Zany Crew of Sentence Constructors
Revised Edition

Linda Smith Masi

Gotham Books

30 N Gould St.
Ste. 20820, Sheridan, WY 82801
https://gothambooksinc.com/

Phone: 1 (307) 464-7800

© 2023 *Linda Smith Masi*. All rights reserved.

No part of this book may be reproduced, stored in a retrieval system, or transmitted by any means without the written permission of the author.

Published by Gotham Books (November 16, 2023)

ISBN: 979-8-88775-370-6 (P)
ISBN: 979-8-88775-371-3 (E)

Because of the dynamic nature of the Internet, any web addresses or links contained in this book may have changed since publication and may no longer be valid.

The views expressed in this work are solely those of the author and do not necessarily reflect the views of the publisher, and the publisher hereby disclaims any responsibility for them.

Credits

"Photo by ©Bibliotheca Alexandrina".

(htto://www.bibalex.org/attachments_en/Gallery/Medium/201002111340166411_BAInauguration.jpg)

Photo by Mohamed Nafea @ Biblioteca Alexandrina

"Photo by © Bibliotheca Alexandrina".

(http://www.bibalex.org/attachments_en/Gallery/Medium/201002111417273608_Rainbow.jpg)

Photo by Mohamed Nafea @ Biblioteca Alexandrina

Unless otherwise shown, all images are copyrighted property of author, © Linda Smith Masi with special appreciation to Giancarmine Nolé www.studionolé.it and to Carolyn Elizabeth Wathen Patterson, Ph. D.

Zanzibar

The Story

A Book About The Sublime Use of Time to Cooperate and Create

**The Library of Alexandria, Egypt of old and of late
Zanzibar and his Zany Crew of Sentence Constructors**

To my mother, Martha Elizabeth Wathen Smith

This book is dedicated to my treasured family:

My husband, Enzo Masi

My children, Douglas Elder and Sarah Hayden

My mother and father, Dr. Loyd and Martha Smith, to whom I am grateful for the gift of school teachers named

Katherine Taylor Howell

And her mother, Irma E. Peterson

Contents
Exercises and Information

Especially ordered for you!
by Zanzibar and his Zany Crew of Sentence Constructors

"Construction begin!" they again chimed in joyously! Zanzibar reminded them that each of them have choices bringing different consequences. "Each of us must play our role but when the story is finally told, it will be we who do decide; hopefully, increasing the joy of this lifetime ride!"

"Sooo," Zanzibar says, "Smile and Begin!!!!!"

Key to Information & Exercises – Illustrations & Conversation

Characters

Zanzibar, the camel	4
Nan Noun, a giraffe	6
Paul Pronoun, a chameleon	8
Veronica Verb, a monkey	9
Anna Adverb, a gazelle	10
Alfred Adjective, an elephant	11
Ike Interjection, a Toucan bird	12
Connie Conjunction, a Chimpanzee	13
Pete Preposition, a zebra	14

Places & Photos

The desert of Egypt	2
Library of Alexandrina, Bibliotheca Alexandrina	20

Key to Exercises for
Zanzibar and his Zany Crew of Sentence Constructors

Information & Question and Answer Page Correlation

The Exercises *Practice Using English*:	Questions Page Number(s):	Answers Page Number(s):
I. Sentences in Books Climbing/Stacking to the Sky!	18 - 19	18 - 19
II. Keywords	21	21
1. W words and How	22	33
2. Identify Which of the 8 Parts of English Speech	23	34
3. Sentence Creation	24 - 25	37 - 38
4. Reading Comprehension	26 - 29	39 - 43
5. Understanding & Analyzing	30	30
6. Five Senses Lesson	31 - 32	31 - 32
The Exercises *Understanding & Using English more easily*	*Page Number(s):*	
Using Essential Words	35	
Subject/Predicate	36	
Rap Song: "Why We've Strived!"	44	

Please review so that we may say, play, to reach a joyful conclusion!

Zanzibar thought, *"I have been crossing this part of the arid land for too long in search of the needed words,"*

Zanzibar listened and smiled at the attention the work was receiving. Tap, tap tap; hammer, hammer, hammer, harder-harder-harder-again and again, as the words fell in:

Anna Adverb asked, "**Where** *should the words ultimately be found?*" *"In their places, both in the books that were and shall be created now,"* said Zanzibar.

Nan Noun announced, "**What** *would be created were the* books *in The Library of Alexandria, the books of the library that had disappeared almost without a trace!*" She added, *"Naturally, now also new books may be written to update the place."* Anna Adverb said, "**When** *was this loss? Way back, more than two thousand years ago, when the world in Alexandria, Egypt was a different place from today in many ways. It was both ruled and attacked by people perhaps only dimly aware or maybe even afraid of how the words could truly serve. This was perhaps before people had a computer capable of uniting and transforming the planet called Earth,"* Anna continued, *"by facilitating the exchange of information; thereby, combining the people of the nations."* She added, "**Why** *was to bring knowledge again to a place where it had been and use the tools to create something new with which to begin again."*

Paul Pronoun said, *"After all, for just* **who** *or* **whom** *are these words intended? They are for all of us in this room of the Universe, our Earth, and also far from it in Outer Space, should there be found collaborators with desire to keep pace with the profound will to create and to participate in the marvel of cooperation."*

Connie Conjunction smiled and said, "**How** *is with patient determination, men could create this paradigm of information and so we could live in the sublime."* *"We could transform the races with all their different colors of faces by sharing and caring."* "**How**," she said, *"would be by knowing and sewing the seeds of harmony."*

Zanzibar said, *"Let's look back at how we began and what we did to arrive at this point." "I remember well,"* he began to reminisce.

Ali, Zanzibar's friend, looked down through his orbit meter into Zanzibar's eyes. The bleak expression did little to encourage him to continue this time journey back to Alexandria, Egypt, the home of the world's greatest library of the time.

"The people in power at the time had chosen him for the daunting task of rebuilding the library's recordings of knowledge."

Surely the years after the loss were a time during which the world's educated people held their breaths hoping that the knowledge lost in the fire at the library could be recovered. All hopes were pinned on **Zanzibar, the camel**, and his zany crew of sentence constructors. Ali saw a tired determined Zanzibar below. Zanzibar felt the cold fetlocks that were opposite his dry mouth and hot burning sweat pouring into his eyes. He thought, I have been crossing this part of the arid land for too long in search of the needed words. Only the small part of his body known as fetlocks were cold and that due to fear. The fire had raged all night in Alexandria and for days afterwards. The precious library, the treasure of its time, had been burned to cinders. Walking through those cinders to find Ali, his friend and former owner, had singed the fur at the position of the fetlocks' encounter with the scorching earth of the Arabian desert. All feeling had been erased by the flames, leaving a strange perception of ice in its place.

No ice could have chilled him more; however, than the realization of the complete destruction of all records of knowledge. The people in power at the time had chosen him for the daunting task of rebuilding the library's records of knowledge. A reconstruction of the building itself would have been a more welcome, less difficult task. To reconstruct every sentence would require a crew of eight specific individuals; eight skilled in their own pursuit of expression; and eight sufficiently skilled and without conceit so that the books could once more become complete. The first one of the crew along with each of the other seven must work well under Zanzibar's direction in order to construct the new and reconstruct the old books in the Library of Alexandria. Reconstruction in the English language had been decided upon in order to take advantage of its synthetic nature which enabled computers to store more concepts using less space than many other languages. The widespread use of English in the modern world had been another reason.

Linda Smith Masi

Nan <u>Noun</u>, a giraffe, . . . *"You can look over the entire sentence with a long neck like that!* **. . .establish the <u>subject</u> . . ."** <u>**"Nouns are the name of something whether it be a person, animal, place or thing."**</u>

"We need to find a representative for each of the **eight** parts of English speech in order to rebuild every sentence," said Zanzibar with a sigh. "Perhaps we should start with a ***noun*** rep and then a ***pronoun*** so that we can easily create ***subjects*** for each sentence." Ali said, "What about action?" Zanzibar replied that verbs would take care of this and could be found after nouns and pronouns. Ali agreed; thereafter, the search was on for subjects—e.g., nouns and pronouns, and the search for action was postponed—e.g., action verbs. At that very moment **Nan <u>Noun</u>**, a <u>giraffe</u> with an incredibly long neck, walked up. Zanzibar stated the obvious, "You can look over the entire sentence with a long neck like that! You can establish the ***<u>subject</u>*** of our sentences in most instances. Will you join us as a noun rep?" "Surely," said Nan, "<u>**Nouns are the name of something whether it be a person, animal, place or thing**</u>." (as highlighted)

Nan and **Zanzibar** worked for several **days** collecting scattered **nouns.** They found structural **parts** of The Library **building** including **nails, planks,** some shattered **windows** and **stone.** Also collected were **bits** of **thread**, from the **seats** of **chairs** upon which **people** once sat to peruse the **books. Nan Noun**, the **giraffe**, diligently carried each **piece** to the collection center according to **Zanzibar's instructions. Nan** also came across many **concepts** and **objects** which were once **nouns** on the **pages** of the **books** scattered by the **fire. Nan** worked diligently transferring **items** able to be **nouns** to the collection **point** while explaining that the **words** and **concepts** were the most important **things** to save.

"**Nouns** to the **fore!**", **Zanzibar** called to start the **participation** in much **creation. Nan Noun** declared that several **subjects** were around to which more **words** needed to be appended when found. The kind, patient **camel** revealed the **pages** waiting to hold **sentences** both new and old, all sparkling with **worth** of **gold.**

See page 36 for more information

Linda Smith Masi

Paul <u>Pronoun</u>, a chameleon, . . . *"Nan, you look tired. Let me help."*
"<u>We pronouns substitute for nouns in the sentences and phrases</u>. . . ."

Soon, **Paul Pronoun**, a **chameleon**, came along and said, "Nan, you look tired. Let me help. We **pronouns substitute for nouns in the sentences and phrases**, especially indicating <u>Who</u>, <u>Whom</u> and <u>What</u> and **sometimes** <u>Which</u>." (as highlighted)

"**This** is a good idea, **I** am becoming tired," said Nan, "thank **you**. But Paul, **you** are looking very drab today." "Oh," Paul Pronoun, replied, "For easy substitution and hiding from predicaments, **we** Chameleons take on the color of **our** environment. Lately, due to the fire, **it** has been dark, smoky and full of soot and **my** look reflects **this**." Nan observed, "Oh, **you** have looked rather drab recently. **Those** are somewhat dull colors." "Yes, **these** are dull, Paul sadly said. Nan smiled at **him**, "When the smoke clears **you** will be bright." **She** wanted the crew to feel good about **themselves** and **their** work.

Zanzibar and his Zany Crew of Sentence Constructors

Veronica <u>Verb</u>, a monkey, ... "...creating the <u>predicate</u>"
<u>*Verbs express action or a mode of being.*</u>

"Well, we certainly cannot go on too much longer without some action— e.g., verbs," said Zanzibar, "<u>***Verbs express action or a mode of being.***</u>" (as highlighted)

Surprisingly, at that very moment, holding a vine, a frisky ***monkey swung*** in on one of her long arms. Zanzibar **said,** "Wow, that **was** a direct reply to my hope for an **action verb** capable of creating the <u>**predicate**</u> of our many sentences." The enthusiastic monkey **jumped** from place to place, **swinging** using one arm and then the other. "Obviously, she can be our verb rep," gleefully exclaimed Zanzibar, "Look at how she creates action!" "What do you mean, verb representative?" asked the monkey. "My name is Veronica," she continued. Zanzibar, smiling, stated the obvious, "Let's call you **Veronica <u>Verb</u>**. Verbs <u>**express action or a mode of being.**</u>"

She **replied,** "I **know** that I **am** good at action; what **is** a mode of being?" Zanzibar enthusiastically **explained,** "If your state; for example, is tired, energetic, happy or sad, just **to name** a few; a verb expressing your state of being is helpful. If Nan **says,** 'I **am** at rest' or 'You **have been** happy,' these statements **illustrate** the point." The frisky monkey **said**, "Ok!, I **see**. For this work **I am** very ready!"

See page 36 for more information

Linda Smith Masi

Anna <u>Adverb</u>, a gazelle,... <u>"Adverbs are words that describe or modify verbs." Questions with which we help are: how & when & where & why</u>.

"Zanzibar," said **Anna, the <u>Adverb</u>**, a **gazelle** signed on for the task of restoring adverbs, "Let's move on, I want to do some **<u>describing or modifying of the verbs</u>** we've found! I want to work with our verb rep. Please fill me in on the details of the **<u>questions with which I can help like: how</u>** and **<u>when</u>** and **<u>where</u>** and **<u>why</u>**. If we need to add to our crew; adverbs are designed to see things **through**." (as highlighted)

Patiently, Zanzibar **slowly** said, "*<u>why</u>* and *<u>how</u>* are so that **soon** we may make complete sentences and paragraphs. Between the four of us; you, Pete, Veronica and me; we can decide *<u>how</u>* and *<u>when</u>* to proceed, **even** answering other questions **speedily**." "We adverbs," Anna **wise*ly*** said, "most **often** answer **how**. If you want to know **how** to construct adverbs," she said, "affix [**ly**] to many words and they **often** become <u>adverbs</u> such as: **wise*ly*, slow*ly*, quick*ly*** or **dangerous*ly*,**" she **happi*ly*** concluded.

Alfred <u>Adjective</u>, an elephant . . . <u>"With your long trunk you can reach **each noun or pronoun** describing or modifying it, often **answering which**."</u>

Down the road **Alfred Elephant** came, his trunk and ears moving slightly in the breeze. When Zanzibar saw his long trunk, he issued him an invitation to sign on for the task of restoring **adjectives. Alfred said,** "Tell me more about your definition of adjectives please." Zanzibar replied, "<u>**Adjectives are words that describe nouns or pronouns; thereby, indicating quality, quantity or something else causing** the **distinction** of a **noun** or **pronoun from something else**</u>." (as highlighted)

Zanzibar continued, "With your **long** trunk, you can reach **each** word in **the** sentence or phrase to give it **a modifying** word telling **the** way it is. Alfred, thinking seriously, asked, "Do you mean describing?" "Your grasp of **the** point is excellent; you may begin. Sometimes you will indicate *which;* for example, *which* one is **the best, worst** or **prettiest** or refer to **an earlier** clause. **An** example is: '**That** boy is **a smart** one, for *which* **the** school awarded him,'" Zanzibar, said with **a broad** grin.

Linda Smith Masi

Ike <u>Interjection</u>, a Toucan bird, . . . "<u>a word or phrase used in exclamation!</u>" . . . "We interjections like to and often do interrupt."

Startling everyone Ike, the <u>Toucan</u>, flew in excitedly and said, "We interjections like to and often do interrupt. We interrupt to exclaim! **<u>Interjections are a word or phrase used in exclamation!</u>"** (as highlighted)

"**<u>Wow</u>! My goodness!** Look at that beak," exclaimed Nan. This colorful Toucan bird originally arrived in Africa from the Amazon, his birthplace, on a ship as a beautiful captive bird. In this new habitat, he had become comfortable. With such gorgeous feathers it was easy to understand why he was given his new home. Screeching with alarm when he saw Connie Conjunction hanging between words, Ike screamed, **"Gosh! My! Oh, no!** She may fall! **Look!,** she is hanging between two words! **Yikes!** He cried out with alarm!"

Zanzibar and his Zany Crew of Sentence Constructors

Connie <u>Conjunction</u>, a Chimpanzee, . . . The purpose of a Conjunction, you see, is to <u>join together words, clauses or phrases</u>.

"No," called out **Connie <u>Conjunction</u>**, the **chimpanzee**, "this job is my calling; my work." She explained, **"<u>The purpose of a Conjunction, you see, is to join together or connect words, clauses or phrases.</u>"** I can help to save space. By using me, many words do not need to be repeated." (as highlighted)

"**So,** please give us an example," said Zanzibar. "OK- Connie wanted to search **and** find, is six words. **Yet** words with the same meaning: Connie wanted to search. Connie wanted to find, is eight words. I'm useful other times but saving space is my most frequent chance to shine."

Linda Smith Masi

Pete <u>Preposition</u>, a zebra, . . . The purpose of a Preposition is to <u>combine with other words, clauses or phrases to indicate relationship or position</u>.

Soon **Pete *Preposition***, a **zebra**, came along, knowing that he represented just who he was – a preppy preposition!" "We **Prepositions** <u>**combine with other words, clauses or phrases;**</u> <u>**combine with nouns, pronouns** or **noun equivalents to** form a *phrase* that has a *relation* with some other word</u>," said Pete Preposition **with** a smile. (as highlighted)

"*I must have an object, in order to be complete;* otherwise, I dangle and fall **off** my feet!" He gleefully said, "I am popular since I must combine every time **for** example, **on** the road, **at** the library, **before** today and **near** the line."

Zanzibar and his Zany Crew of Sentence Constructors

<u>Interjections</u> *interrupt often exclaiming and explaining.*

Excited, Ike interjected, "Like driving a car **on** the street. To drive a car your driving must be neat!" I repeat, "Your driving must be neat!" "Yes," **exclaimed** Ike, "It is **imperative, <u>very necessary,</u>** that your driving be organized and neat." Interjections interrupt often exclaiming and explaining. Then Ike asked, "Where do we write **declarative, interrogative, exclamatory** or **imperative** sentences?"

Zanzibar replied, "A **<u>declarative</u>** form must be created when <u>*information is to be stated.*</u> These sentences are fun to create because they're full of ideas, things, hopes and dreams. Constructing a paragraph or phrase? A **<u>declarative</u>** form is often the first choice of the day! If a <u>*question needs to be asked*</u> use an **<u>interrogative</u>** form for the task. *If surprise, horror or delight is an element*, the exclamatory form is just excellent." If you <u>just must</u> say, the **imperative** form will give you a way. It matters not if our sentences are simple, compound, complex or compound-complex, each of them will fall within on of the following categories: declarative, interrogative, exclamatory or imperative." cawed **Ike <u>Interjection.</u>**

Linda Smith Masi

"OK, he thought, the eight parts of speech have been identified."

Later, Zanzibar, reposing on the sand, saw and heard the eight representatives of the English language assembled all together, working in symmetry. Here the crew reminds me of a marching band, he thought, wherein every person and instrument is complementary to the group for creating beauty or cacophony. The words of the crew drifted through the air as he watched and listened. "We must succeed you know," said Nan Noun. "It is important for our world to avoid the desolation which often occurs in the presence of isolation," added Alfred Adjective. He continued, "A library can very much help to enlighten people." Veronica Verb spoke, "Without this effort of creation to save the books; the ideas, concepts, facts and perceptions expressed therein may not reach an accurate realization." Ike Interjection interjected, "Yes, the enormous effort of our forebear and the energy they spent to enlighten, needs to be known to augment our day." "Also, to save this awareness for more than solitary fame for more than just making a name," Paul Pronoun solemnly stated. Connie Conjunction suggested, "All of us can use this enlightenment now to become the

Basis for the people of the world to avoid isolation and to enjoy the act of creative cooperation." Anna Adverb smiled and said, "We shall work together to achieve our goal." Pete Preposition formally announced, "The Library of Alexandria and her precious contents shall stand like a shining pearl for our Earth to have once more."

"To work!" Nan Noun and Zanzibar exclaimed simultaneously. We do need to begin construction. What kind of sentences do we need to construct?, he pondered. We need **declarative** and **interrogative**, **imperative** and **exclamatory** sentences, he realized with satisfaction. The eight members of the zany crew of sentence constructors were gathered around him and agreed.

Nan asked, "Talk about forming **interrogative** sentences please." Zanzibar replied, "When we have questions; when we are unsure of how, we should ask questions as to *who* and *how* and *which* and *why* and *where* and *when* in order to get a lead. A lead is often the subject of a sentence or phrase that can lead us up high!" "Yes," said Veronica Verb, "**interrogative** sentences lead us climbing, stacking to the sky! Each of them are punctuated with a **question mark [?].**" Ever curious Connie Chimpanzee asked, "What does punctuated mean?" Zanzibar explained that to best know what words mean, we must understand the order and meaning via traffic signals called **punctuation**. For example, a **period [.]** at the end of a sentence indicates that it is time to stop. A **question mark** [?] at the end means that an answer; hopefully, is on its way. An **exclamation point** [!] often pours excitement into the joint, whether we be at the opera or the beach or in our bedrooms dreaming while fast asleep. A **colon** [:] suggests that a list follows next. A **semicolon** [;] reminds us to pause a bit and then continue to convey our meaning. Within the phrase, a **comma** [,] or two can save the day by reminding us to take a break along the way. An **asterisk** [*], of course, refers to something written somewhere else. "What about **parenthesis** [(...)]?" Connie asked. "Oh yes," Zanzibar replied, "a bit like commas, two parenthesis provide a chance to give more information or to set apart something less important. Without them many times the words would remain dark and unseen. Actually, they can help keep things very clean."

Said the zany crew, "We understand **declarative** sentences announce who, what, why, where, how and when. Suddenly, we know how to explain, how to describe, how and why! **Imperative** sentences give us a sense of urgency. **Exclamatory** sentences provide a sense of intensity." Zanzibar exclaimed, "Oh, yes! And if you have questions just use an **interrogative** form to let us know. We can answer even if we are on the go. Each of these English sentences may be one of the four types: simple, complex, compound or even compound-complex. All are valid and our response to provide them can be rapid."

"**Now,**" said Zanzibar, "it is time to begin." Rat-a-tat-tat, the words began to fall into the sentences and phrases just like that! One by one the words followed the direction of Zanzibar. He knew where they should be and were. He said, "**Nouns to the fore!**" **Nan Noun**, the giraffe, proudly walked to the front followed by a collection of nouns soon to be found in books of the Library. On her heels came **Paul Pronoun**, the chameleon; there to be sure that Nan did not tire. **Veronica Verb**, the busy monkey, brought her group of verbs. **Alfred Adjective**, the elephant, and **Anna Adverb**, the gazelle, were present to modify and describe. Of course; **Connie Conjunction**, **Pete Preposition** and **Ike Interjection** were there to make sure that no one messed around. Just look at these sentences: the construction is done! As in the first four, you add example lines from the other titles and all will be won!

Sentences in Books Climbing/Stacking to the Sky!

Romeo and Juliet by William Shakespeare

"Good-night, good-night! Parting is such sweet sorrow..."
"adj-noun, adj-noun! noun verb adv adj noun...."
Juliet, Act II, scene ii

Red Sorghum by Mo Yan, pen name of Guan Moye

"The sorghum is red—the Japanese are coming—compatriots,..."
"adj noun verb adj—adj Proper noun verb noun—noun,..."

Dr. Zhivago by Boris Pasternak

"You and I, it's as though we have been taught to kiss in heaven *pron.conj. pron. pron'verb(cnt conj.conj.pron, verb verb verb prep* and sent down to earth together, ..."
verb prep noun conj verb adv prep noun adverb

The Divine Comedy by Dante Alighieri

"The darkest places in hell are reserved for those who maintain *adj adj noun prep noun verb verb prep adv adv verb* their neutrality in times of moral crisis."
pron noun prep noun prep adj noun

The Id and The Ego by Sigmund Freud

The Miser by Moliere

Don Quixote by Miguel de Cervantes

Spring Snow by Yukio Mishima

The Critique of Pure Reason by Immanuel Kant

---

100 Years of Solitude by Gabriel Garcia Marquez

Zanzibar and his Zany Crew of Sentence Constructors

<u>The Son of Two Civilizations</u> by Naguib Mahfouz

<u>The Old Man and The Sea</u> by Ernest Hemingway

<u>Shosha</u> by Isaac B. Singer

<u>The Iliad</u> by Homer

Old Classics For Children:
<u>The Bobbsey Twins</u> by Edward Stratmayer

Old Classics For Children:
<u>Horton Hatches the Egg</u> by Theodor Seuss Greisel

Zanzibar said, "These are just to name a few."

Nevertheless, Ike Interjection, being himself, screamed, "<u>I</u> want to go first." Connie Conjunction burst in, "I want to connect, take me first, not him!" Calmly, Zanzibar reminded them that subjects come first in order to establish the topic without which all of them should just forget "So, let's see what the nouns have to say," Paul Pronoun smiled, "I will come afterwards to be sure that nothing, due to fatigue, is left behind." Zanzibar announced, "The modern library is electronic. The books are stored as data!" "Why?" asked Connie. Zanzibar replied, "This way, you see, information can be shared easily via the internet."

"Now that all of you are signed in," said Zanzibar, "I want to be sure that everyone really understands. Look into the future and see what a marvelous situation in which we are given the chance to be; to participate and to create. Look into the time machine, see the year 2002, the year the Library opened again for me and for you. Yes, it is far ahead, but if we keep our wits about us, this act of cooperation may become the norm! Just take a look."

Photo by Mohamed Nafea © Bibliotheca Alexandrina

Photo by Mohamed Nafea © Bibliotheca Alexandrina

"The Library is so beautifully lit," they all breathed in a sigh. "Look again, there is more," said Zanzibar. "Do you see the rainbow that appeared? This is the symbol of a promise, you know. There is much to do, let us begin!"

Keywords

1. Adjective
2. Adverb
3. Africa
4. Alexander the Great
5. Alexandria, Egypt
6. Basis
7. Camel
8. Chimpanzee
9. Communicate
10. Conjunction
11. Cooperation
12. Cornerstone
13. Egypt
14. Elephant
15. English
16. English Phrase
17. Gazelle
18. Giraffe
19. Grammar
20. Interjection
21. Library
22. Monkey
23. Noun
24. Parts of Speech
25. Preposition
26. Pronoun
27. Rules of English
28. Sentence Construction
29. Sentence Formation
30. Sentence Structure
31. Take a Break
32. Toucan Bird
33. Verb
34. Zebra

W words and *How* Exercise

A new Library of Alexandria is constructed. It holds much information digitally. It is so because, due to the internet, it is easy to share information with all in the world with interest and access to equipment.

Answer the questions below by underlining the **best** answer:

1. **What** is constructed?
    a) A swimming pool
    b) The Library in Alexandria, Egypt
    c) A new hotel

2. **Where** is it located?
    a) Alexandria, Egypt
    b) Alexandria, Virginia, USA
    c) Shanghai, China

3. **When** is it available to people to use?
    a) Yesterday/ Then
    b) Today/ Now
    c) Tomorrow/ Later

4. **Who** constructed the first Library of Alexandria? ***Subject Form:***
    a) Alexander the Great
    b) Napoleon
    c) Queen Elizabeth

5. **Who** was present at the opening ceremony? ***Object Form:***
    a) Present were many interested people, all of whom have interest in the story of the Library.
    b) A friend of the first Emperor of China
    c) People from the country of Turkey

6. **How** is data stored in the Modern Library of Alexandria?
    a) On paper
    b) On stone
    c) Digitally

Answers on page 33 & Relates to information on pages 30 & 35

Identify Which of the Eight (8) Parts of English Speech

Write in the space the name of *which* of the eight parts of English speech the underlined word in each sentence represents:

I. My! the **Library** certainly contains information about many topics and places.
    Which of the eight (8) parts of English speech is the word **Library** in the sentence above?
    In this sentence, the word **Library** is a _____.

II. My! **It** certainly contains information about many topics and places.
    Which of the eight parts of English speech is the word **It** in the sentence above?
    In this sentence, the word **It** is a _____.

III. My! The Library certainly **contains** information about many topics and places.
    Which of the eight parts of English speech is the word **contains** in the sentence above?
    In this sentence, the word **contains** is a _____.

IV. My! The Library certainly contains **much** information about many topics and places.
    Which of the eight parts of English speech is the word **much** in the sentence above?
    In this sentence, the word **much** is an _____.

V. My! The Library **certainly** contains much information about many topics and places.
    Which of the eight parts of English speech is the word **certainly** in the sentence above?
    In this sentence, the word **certainly** is an _____.

VI. My! The Library certainly contains much information **about** many topics and places.
    Which of the eight parts of English speech is the word **about** in the sentence above?
    In this sentence, the word **about** is a _____.

VII. My! The Library certainly contains much information about many topics **and** places.
    Which of the eight parts of English speech is the word **and** in the sentence above?
    In this sentence, the word **and** is a _____.

VIII. **My**! The Library certainly contains much information about many topics and places.
    Which of the eight parts of English speech is the word **My** in the sentence above?
    In this sentence, the word **My** is an _____.

Answers on page 34

Sentence Creation

From the words beneath each sentence choose the one that best completes the sentence. Be sure to choose the **best answer**.

I. NOUNS

    1) In the story the _____ are working on books for The Modern Library of Alexandria.
        a) animals   b) cars   c) machines
    2) The work is on the _____ of The Library of Alexandria.
        a) corn   b) books   c) swimming pool
    3) The work is on The _____ of Alexandria.
        a) Hospital   b) Library   c) Zoo

II. PRONOUNS

    1) The Library of Alexandria is ready for visitors. _____ is an interesting place.
        a) They   b) We   c) It

    2) Zanzibar is a camel. _____ is in charge of the project to reconstruct the Library books.
        a) It   b) He   c) They

    3) If you write a book for the Library, you can say, "_____ wrote his book."
        a) I   b) Her   c) It

III. VERBS

    1) To _____ a new place we must open our eyes.
        a) color   b) write   c) see

    2) Where we live _____ our home.
        a) drives   b) is   c) dances

    3) Hot weather _____ in summer in most places.
        a) arrives   b) eats   c) sleeps

IV. ADJECTIVES

    1) The hat is _____ .
        a) black   b) dog   c) eat

    2) A horse is not _____ .
        a) green   b) tall   c) circular

3) Where is the _____ boy two years old?
    a) old   b) young   c) girl

V. ADVERBS

1) How _____ the time passes!
    a) red   b) quickly   c) slowly

2) Where are the _____ grazing sheep?
    a) calmly   b) dancing   c) horses

3) The ant crosses the street _____ .
    a) which   b) jogging   c) slowly

VI. CONJUNCTIONS

1) John _____ Anne dance together.
    a) stars   b) and   c) they

2) Mary likes hamburgers _____ no onions.
    a) but   b) galaxies   c) both

3) The mother gave the children milk _____ no honey.
    a) stars   b) we   c) but

VII. PREPOSITIONS

1) When we want a fish we go _____ a store.
    a) eat   b) to   c) on

2) After the game the players go _____ their bus to go home.
    a) their   b) joke   c) onto

3) _____ the Rainbow is a nice song.
    a) <u>Over</u>   b) <u>Red</u>   c) <u>Telephone</u>

VIII. INTERJECTIONS

1) _____ she looks great!
    a) Wow,   b) Horse,   c) Sad

2) The crow caws loudly, _____ he is noisy!
    a) my   b) serious,   c) birthday,

3) _____ It is hard to believe.
    a) Wow!   b) Only!   c) Late!

Answers on pages 37 - 38

Reading Comprehension

Questions for students
Please read and answer the following:

Without a framework, a building will fall. Without a skeleton, a body will not be able to stand. Without a theme; a story, movie, piece of ballet, work of art, literature, opera or business providing jobs, inventions and products may not develop in a sustainable way. By understanding the framework with which the English language conveys meaning, our communication using it is enhanced. Our words may stand and grow. We have the possibility of enjoying our lives together all the more and so, please read ahead and participate.

The following are explanations of the eight parts of English speech. The explanations are followed by questions.

In the following, read the words and answer the questions that follow: (Note: The answers, if objective, should be underlined.) In the extra space write a sentence about one of the characters in the book using the part of speech just explained. This is your opportunity to change the outcome of the story.

I. Nan **Noun** arrived displaying a parade of nouns including the building materials: fiber-optic wire and cable, glass, nails, sheets of aluminum and stainless steel. Every building element was shown. **A noun name and is often the subject of a sentence or phrase**.

   A. **What** is being displayed according to the **paragraph** above from the **book, Zanzibar and his Zany Crew of Sentence Constructors?**

   _____

   B. **What part** of English speech are the **words: materials, wire, cable, glass, nails, foam** and metal **sheets**?

   _____

Your sentence: _____

II. Veronica **Verb** and a parade of verbs enjoy and like to come and march along. **A verb demonstrates action or a state of being** She shows the reconstruction of the Library. With her **are** a group of verbs who **like** to **decide, choose, measure, hammer, nail, participate, create** and **build**.

   A. Why is the question correct even though stating, smiling, building, participating and creating are not proceeded by the words, to be?

   _____

B. What part of speech are the words: being, deciding, measuring, choosing, hammering, nailing, laughing, stating, smiling, building, participating and creating?

_____

Your sentence: _____

III. Paul **Pronoun** came and announced, this is what life should be all about. I am here to be sure that Nan Noun does not fall around. I will replace her when she needs to lie down. After all, pronouns know many solutions because we have the privilege of substitution. Most likely you know that we have different forms and may be complicated: —in subject form: <u>I, we, you, you, he, she, it, they, and who</u> or to put it another way, in object form: <u>me, them, you, us, him, her, it, us, whom</u>. We also have <u>possessive</u>, <u>reflexive</u>, some <u>situations</u> <u>with</u> <u>gerunds</u> and those often confusing: Who and Whom, Your and You're, Its and It's, Whose and Who's. Those shall be dealt with another time."

A. Write two (2) sentences using a ***subject form*** of ***pronoun*** substituting for the noun, coffee.
For example: <u>Coffee</u> tastes good. **Some people think that *it* tastes even better than tea.**

Your sentences:

1. _____

2. _____

B. Write two (2) sentences using the ***object form*** of **pronoun** substituting for the noun, cookies.
For example: When **I** come home hungry, **I** always eat <u>cookies</u>.
Some people think **there** is nothing better than ***them***.

Your sentences:

1. _____

2. _____

IV. Anna <u>Adverb</u> and her group of <u>adverbs</u> ending in *<u>ly</u>* (pronounced reminded them that not every word ending in *<u>ly</u>* is an adverb but many are so. **Some** of Anna Adverb's words are: **lovingly, happily, quickly, wisely, warmly, sadly** and **excitedly**. Zanzibar said, "Tell me, Anna, exactly what you adverbs really can contribute please." Anna practically chirped, she was so excited by his question. "We adverbs often answer, **How**,' she continued, '**wisely, deliberately,** or **quickly, securely** or

dangerously. When we are in use *ly* often appears at the end of words. We also often answer *when.*"'

    A. **When** the crew met together, do you think they were **decidedly** united in **how** to construct the new books of The Library?

        _____

    B. What part of speech are the words: lovingly, happily, quickly, wisely, sadly and excitedly?

        _____

Your sentence: _____

V. Alfred **Adjective** arrived with a group of adjectives interested in giving their description of some nouns and pronouns. He brought along: beautiful, exquisite, digital, interesting, happy, sad, tall, short, long, red, green, black, white, beautiful and horrible. "Adjectives are required when describing things, and there are just too may to bring them all," said Alfred.

    A. The Modern Library is built on the Mediterranean Sea. Many agree that the Sea is a sparkling jewel like the Library. Write why you think the Library is built on the Mediterranean Sea?

        _____

    B. Using adjectives, describe an aspect of the Library of which you are aware.

        _____

Your sentence: _____

VI. Zanzibar said, "Pete, please bring some friends to help us introduce." Pete **Preposition** soon led a line of prepositions introducing topics. Singing a song, the group coming along included: of, to, in, at, about, over, above and on. Zanzibar explained that these powerful, little words are essential in sentence creation.

    A. In the sentences write an appropriate preposition:
        1) The Library is (____) the Mediterranean Sea. She looked (____) the sea often.

        2) The clock rang seven times (____) the morning and I awakened and went (____) the Library.

    B. Choose the best preposition for the following sentences or phrases from the choices shown after the sentences:
        1) The digital nature (____) the Library is helpful in communicating with people (____) the world. [of, on, in]

2) Perhaps the digital aspect the (___) Library can help communication all (___) the world. [from, of, over]

Your sentence: _____

VII. Connie **Conjunction**, always connecting, asked, "Where is this Library *and* where is it built? Remember words used to connect other words or phrases are conjunctions," she explained. Look at the sentences below for examples.

- It was built in Alexandria, Egypt and is located there.
- It is located on the Mediterranean Sea *but* not on the Red Sea.

A. What words in the two sentences above are conjunctions?

_____

B. Which words in the following sentences are conjunctions?
To answer underline the conjunctions in the sentences below:
The boys alone went to the dance as a group but they were hopeful of meeting girls. Regrettably, no girls both single and without a date were present.

_____

Your sentence: _____

VIII. Ike **Interjection** cawed, "We finished! The building is complete. Now we need to always be alert for any changes to Interjections inject information into a story." keep it so.

A. Write sentences that may have been spoken at the time of the fire thousands of years ago using an Interjection.

_____ or:

_____

B. Write a sentence explaining **Why** you think that a toucan bird is the representative for interjections?

_____

_____

Your sentence: _____

Answers on pages 39 - 43

Need to understand or analyze?
Try the below and you'll be surprised!:
Questions Using **Who?, What?, When?, Where? and Why?**
Can help us understand. **This** and **That** and their plurals:
These and **Those** are helpful too.
Knowing **How** may be the biggest assist or help of all.

1. **Who** thought of the idea of a Library in Alexandria long ago?
   That was the idea of King **Alexander the Great**.

2. **What** creative idea was thought of long ago that helped lead men to enlightenment?
   That was the idea of a great library in Alexandria, Egypt.

3. **When** did it first open? **That** was a very **long time ago**. It was destroyed in a fire; and later rebuilt. **When** did the Modern Library of Alexandria open?
   This opened in 2002.

4. **Where** was the old and is the new Library located?
   It was and is in **Alexandra, Egypt**. **This** is the home of it.

5. **Why** is the Library important?
   It is important because in the past it has helped spread awareness and continues to enlighten today.

6. **How** is the **information stored** and **shared** in the Modern Library of Alexandria?
   It is stored and shared **digitally**. These modern records and those ancient records are stored in a way that they may be easily shared.

Relates to information on pages 22 & 35

**The effort of recreating the Library in such a sharing, caring way
fulfills the hope of enlightenment
King Alexander the Great so wanted to foster long ago.**

Come and enjoy!

Zanzibar and his Zany Crew of Sentence Constructors

"Zanzibar," said Ike interjection, "all of us want to learn how to state what we see, hear, touch, smell and taste. Will you teach us?," he continued. "Oh, yes," said the camel, feeling very important. "We need to discuss the five senses, Zanzibar explained, please see the lesson below."

The Five Senses Lesson
What are the five senses?

They are: Sight, Sound, Touch, Smell, Taste

Each sense has two components. The first is the act of using the sense, as shown in the column on the left below. The second component is the user's action and/or reaction to the experience of using the sense as shown in the column on the right below:

1. Sight (n):
Note:
to *watch* indicates *action*—e.g., I watch the bird fly.
to look indicates that the observed in with or with *very little or no movement*, i.e. I look at the bird sitting it on the nest.

To See (v)   To Look/Watch (v)

I see the bird.   **I watch** the bird.   **I look** at the bird.
You see the bird.   **You watch** the bird.   **You look** at the bird.
He, She, It sees the bird. **He watches** the bird.   **She watches** the bird.
I see the bird in the sky.   I watch it fly.
    I see and look at the bird sitting on the nest. She does not move.

"Because I have a long neck, I can see many things all around," said Nan Noun, the giraffe.

2. Sound (n):

To Hear (v)   To Listen (v)

I hear the sound of birds singing.   **I listen** to the sound of birds singing.

Alfred Elephant added, "My big ears enable me to hear everything very well."

3. Touch (n):

To Touch (v)   To Feel (v)

I touch the soft grass.   **I feel** the soft grass.

When I touch the concrete it feels rough and hurts me. Ike Interjection screamed, "I can touch just about everything because my wings take me where I want to go."

4. Smell (n):

To Smell (v)   To recognize (v)   To like (v)
I smell the rose.   **I recognize** the scent of the rose.   **I like** the scent of the rose

When I smell the roses I recognize the scent of them. I like the smell.

Veronica Verb suggested, "To smell a rose is as much fun as smelling perfume."

5. Taste (n):

To taste (v)   To enjoy (v)   To like (v)
I taste the flavor(flavour).   **I enjoy** the taste.   **I like**

Pete Preposition, the preppy zebra, declared, "Taste has two meanings!" "It may refer to the flavor of a food or drink but it may also refer to the style with which one dresses, speaks and behaves." "Please notice my always stylish look and behavior." Anna Adverb said, "I especially like your bow tie." "Thank you, Anna," replied Pete.

Below write a sentence using each one of the five senses:

1.

2.

3.

4.

5.

W words and *How* - Answer Key

Answers are underlined and shown in **bold** below:

A new Library of Alexandria is constructed. It holds much information digitally. It is so because, due to the internet, it is easy to share information with all in the world who have interest and access to equipment.

Answer the questions below by choosing the **best** answer: (the tense of the verb is a clue to the answer)

1. **What** is constructed?
    a) A swimming pool
    b) The Modern Library of Alexandria, Egypt
    c) A new hotel

2. **Where** is it located?
    a) Alexandria, Egypt
    b) Alexandria, Virginia, USA
    c) Shanghai, China

3. **When** is it available to people to use?
    a) Yesterday
    b) Today/now
    c) Tomorrow

4. **Who** constructed the first Library of Alexandria? *Subject Form:*
    a) Alexander the Great
    b) Napoleon
    c) Queen Elizabeth

5. **Who** was present at the opening ceremony? *Object Form:*
    a) Present were many interested people, all of whom have interest in the story of The Library.
    b) A friend of the first Emperor of China
    c) People from the country of Turkey

6. **How** is data stored in the Modern Library of Alexandria?
    a) On paper
    b) On stone
    c) Digitally

Questions on page 22 & Relates to information on pages 30 & 35

Identify Which of the Eight (8) Parts of English Speech - Answer Key

Write the name of which one of the eight parts of English speech the underlined word in each sentence represents:

I. My! The **Library** certainly contains information about many topics and places.
. . . Which of the eight (8) parts of English speech is the word **Library** in the sentence above?
. . . In this sentence, the word **Library** is a _____**noun**_____.

II. My! **It** certainly contains information about many topics and places
. . . Which of the eight parts of English speech is the word **It** in the sentence above?
. . . In this sentence, the word **It** is a _____**pronoun**_____.

III. My! The Library certainly **contains** information about many topics and places.
. . . Which of the eight parts of English speech is the word **contains** in the sentence above?
. . . In this sentence, the word **contains** is a _____**verb**_____.

IV. My! The Library certainly contains **much** information about many topics and places.
. . . Which of the eight parts of English speech is the word **much** in the sentence above?
. . . In this sentence, the word **much** is an _____**adjective**_____.

IV. My! The Library **certainly** contains much information about many topics and places.
. . . Which of the eight parts of English speech is the word **certainly** in the sentence above?
. . . In this sentence, the word **certainly** is an _____**adverb**_____.

V. My! The Library certainly contains much information **about** many topics and places.
. . . Which of the eight parts of English speech is the word **about** in the sentence above?
. . . In this sentence, the word **about** is a _____**preposition**_____.

VI. My! The Library certainly contains much information about many topics **and** places.
. . . Which of the eight parts of English speech is the word **and** in the sentence above?
. . . In this sentence, the word **and** is a _____**conjunction**_____.

VII. **My!** The Library certainly contains much information about many topics and places.
. . . Which of the eight parts of English speech is the word **My** in the sentence above?
. . . In this sentence, the word **My** is an _____**interjection**_____.

Questions on page 23

Comprehending English more Easily
Topic: Understanding using essential words

I. Understanding how to use the answers to the six underlined words below helps with comprehension.

"How may we understand the words in a paragraph?" Nan asked Zanzibar. With his wisdom on display, Zanzibar did say, "Knowing the answers to the six underlined words below often provides a reliable road."

1. **How** - is often an adverb explaining in what manner or way—e.g., explaining how we can create the best books today.

2. **Why** - is often an adverb asking for what cause, reason or purpose, e.g., why were the books of the Library reconstructed? They were reconstructed to bring knowledge again to a place where it had been and use the books to create something new with which to begin again.

3. **What** - is often a pronoun used like a question to inquire about an object or matter-e.g., *what* part of speech is the word how in the following: They were deciding how to build the new library. How is an adverb.

4. **When** - is often an adverb asking at what time or on what date-e.g., *when* did the modern Library of Alexandria open? In *what* year did it open? The modern Library opened officially in the year 2002.

5. **Who** - is often a pronoun asking what or which person/ persons-e.g., *who* was present at the opening ceremony? Present at the opening were many interested people including government officials, writers, historians, film makers, actors, actresses and others, all of whom have interest in the Library.

6. **Where** - is often a noun indicating placement- *Where* is the library located? It is located in Alexandria, Egypt on the coast of the Mediterranean Sea.

Relates to Exercises on page 22 & Information, page 30

Topic: Subject/Predicate

Without a subject and a predicate we do not have a sentence. Every sentence has a *topic* or *subject* and *verb* or *predicate*.

Nouns are often words serving as the subject or topic of a sentence. Many times they answer the questions who or what. They announce the subject. "You see, Nan proudly explained, 'noun is even in the word announce!'" Ike screeched, "Wow! It's true, look at announce!" "Names, are always capitalized because they are proper nouns," said Zanzibar solemnly. Pete Preposition, with a new bow tie, agreed and boasted, "Look at me, how much more proper can one be!" Smiling, Nan Noun displayed a parade of building materials including fiber optic wire, stainless steel, computer chips, glass and nails to be used in constructing The Library. Also needed, of course, were the texts of thoughts and ideas often in the form of books. When English is used, each word is one of the eight parts of English sentences and phrases. Essential are the nouns mentioned above in the reconstruction of the building and the sentences.

Verbs are often words serving as the predicate of a sentence expressing the action or state of being of the subject. Sometimes we take a verb and talk about the action as though it were a noun. For instance, sometimes we have VERBS- ABLE TO ACT AS NOUNS when we are discussing action or condition. For example, "I love you." Love is the predicate. It expresses what I do. We can also say, "Love is a beautiful thing." With a smile, Connie blushed and softly said, "That turned our verb into the topic of the sentence." Ike Interjection cawed: "Sometimes we even add *ing* to a verb to make it behave like a noun." "What do you mean?", said Connie. Ike replied, "Well, *run* is a verb. It shows action but running is a noun." Nan said, "Wow, we may use it as a subject. Since I am so often the subject, this would give me time to rest." Paul Pronoun, Anna Adverb, Alfred Adjective, Connie Conjunction, Pete Preposition and Ike Interjection, feeling unimportant, asked sadly, "What about us?" Veronica explained, "These simple sentences can be so boring. We do need all of you other words or we may fall asleep. We need you to describe and add interest to the nouns and verbs."

See pages 26 - 29 more information on pages: 39 - 43

Sentence Creation – Answer Key

From the words beneath each sentence choose the one that best completes the sentence. Be sure to choose the **best answer.**

I. NOUNS

    1) In the story the ____**a)**____ are working on the books for The Modern Library of Alexandria.
        a) animals   b) cars   c) machines

    2) The work is on the ____**b)**____ of The Library of Alexandria.
        a) corn   b) books   c) swimming pool

    3) The work is on The ____**b)**____ of Alexandria.
        a) Hospital   b) Library   c) Zoo

II. PRONOUNS

    1) The Library of Alexandria is ready for visitors. ____**c)**____ Is an interesting place.
        a) They   b) We   c) It

    2) Zanzibar is a camel. ____**b)**____ is in charge of the project. To reconstruct the Library books.
        a) It   b) He   c) They

    3) If you write a book for the Library, you can say, " ____**a)**____
        a) I   b) Her   c) It

III. VERBS

    1) To ____**c)**____ a new place we must open our eyes.
        a) color   b) write   c) see

    2) Where we live ____**b)**____ our home.
        a) drives   b) is   c) dances

    3) Hot weather ____**a)**____ in summer in most places.
        a) arrives   b) eats   c) sleeps

IV. ADJECTIVES

    1) The hat is ____**a)**____ .
        a) black   b) dog   c) eat

    2) A horse is not ____**a)**____ .

      a) green   b) tall   c) circular

   3) Where is the __**b)**__ boy two years old?
      a) old   b) young   c) girl

V. ADVERBS

   1) How __**b)**__ the time passes !
      a) red   b) quickly   c) slowly

   2) Where are the __**a)**__ grazing sheep?
      a) calmly   b) dancing   c) horses

   3) The ant crosses the street __**c)**__ .
      a) which   b) jogging   c) slowly

VI. CONJUNCTIONS

   1) John __**b)**__ Anne dance together.
      a) stars   b) and   c) they

   2) Mary likes hamburgers __**a)**__ no onions.
      a) but   b) galaxies   c) both

VII. PREPOSITIONS

   1) When we want a fish we go __**b)**__ a store.
      a) eat   b) to   c) on

   2) After the game the players go __**c)**__ their bus to go home.
      a) their   b) joke   c) onto

   3) __**a)**__ the Rainbow is a nice song.
      a) <u>Over</u>   b) <u>Red</u>   c) <u>Telephone</u>

VIII. INTERJECTIONS

   1) __**a)**__ she looks great!
      a) Wow,   b) Horse,   c) Sad,

   2) The crow caws loudly, __**a)**__ he is noisy!
      a) my,   b) serious,   c) birthday,

   3) __**a)**__ It is hard to believe.
      a) Wow!   b) Horse!   c) Late!

<u>Questions on pages 24 - 25</u>

Reading Comprehension - Answer Key

Answers shown in **bold**
Please read and answer the following:

The following are explanations of the eight parts of English speech. They are followed by questions. In the following sentences read the words and answer the questions that follow: (Note: The answers, if objective, are in **bold**.) In the extra space write a sentence about one of the characters using the part of speech just explained.

I. Nan **Noun** arrived displaying a parade of **nouns** including the building materials: fiber-optic wire and cable, glass, nails, foam, sheets of aluminum and stainless steel. Shown was every building element. **A noun names and is often the subject of a sentence or phrase.**

   A. In the **paragraph** above **what** is being displayed?
   Building **materials** are being displayed.
   What part of English speech are the words: materials, wire, cable, glass, nails, sheets aluminum and stainless steel?

   A. **What** part of English **speech** are the **words: materials, wire, cable, glass, nails, sheets?**
   Each **one** of the **words** listed is a **noun**.

   Your sentence: _____

II. Veronica **Verb** and a parade of verbs came marching along. Veronica was enjoying demonstrating the action and the state of being they were producing. She was showing a group of verbs being, deciding, measuring, choosing, hammering, nailing, laughing, stating, smiling, building, participating and creating.

   A. Why is the above paragraph correct though the words: **decide, choose, measure, hammer, nail, participate, create, build** are proceeded by the words, to be? What tense are these verbs? **The reason is because the words to be are implicit and do not need to be repeated. The verbs are in the present tense.**

   B. What part of speech and in what tense are the words: decided, **chose, measured, hammered, nailed, participated, created** and **built**? Which of the above eight words forms the past tense irregularly? **The verbs are in the past tense. Chose and built are irregular in the past tense.** Regularly to form the past tense only *ed* is added.

   The words are verbs.

Your sentence: _____

39

III. Paul **Pronoun** came and announced, "This is what life should be all about. I am here to be sure that Nan Noun does not fall around. I will replace her when she needs to lie down. After all, pronouns know many solutions because we have the privilege of substitution. Most likely you know that we have different forms and may be complicated: —in subject form: I, we, you, you, he, she, it, they, and who or to put it another way, in object form: me, them, you, us him, her, it, us, whom. We also have possessive, reflexive, some situations with gerunds and those often confusing: Who and Whom, Your and You're, Its and It's, Whose and Who's. Those shall be dealt with another time."

   A. Write two (2) sentences using a *subject form* of *pronoun* substituting for the noun, coffee.
   For example: *Coffee* tastes good. Some people think that it tastes even better with sugar.
   Your sentences may be:
   Coffee brews well in a pot. ***It brews well in a pot.***
   Tom likes the *coffee* when served with sugar. **He likes *it* when served with sugar.**

   B. Write two (2) sentences using the *object form* of *pronoun* substituting for the noun, cookies.
   For example:
   When **I** come home hungry, **I** always eat cookies.
   Some people think **there** is nothing better than ***them.***
   Your sentences may be:
   It is really fun to eat *cookies*. **I** *enjoy* eating ***them***.

Finding the *cookies* may be difficult if they are hidden.
Finding *them* may be difficult if they are hidden.

1. Your sentence _____

2. Your sentence _____

IV. Anna **Adverb** and her group of adverbs ending in *ly* (pronounced reminded them that not every word ending in *ly* is an adverb but many are so. Some of Anna Adverb's words are: lovingly, happily, quickly, wisely, warmly, sadly and excitedly. Zanzibar said, "Tell me, Anna, just exactly what you what you adverbs do contribute. Anna practically chirped, she was so excited by his great question. "We adverbs often answer, 'How,' she continued, 'wisely, slowly or quickly, securely or dangerously. When we are in use *ly* often appears at the end of words. We also often answer *when*."'

   A. When the crew met together, do you think they were decidedly united in how to construct the new books of The Library?
   They were decidedly united in *how* to construct the new books of Library.

Zanzibar and his Zany Crew of Sentence Constructors

B. What part of speech are the words: lovingly, happily, quickly, wisely, sadly and excitedly?
    They are adverbs.

Your sentence _____

V. Alfred **Adjective** arrived with a following of <u>adjectives</u> interested in giving their description of some nouns and pronouns. He brought along: beautiful, exquisite, digital, interesting, happy, sad, tall, short, long, red, green, black, white, beautiful and horrible. "Adjectives are required when describing things, and there are just too many to bring them all," said Alfred.

   A. The Modern Library is built on the Mediterranean Sea. Many agree that the Sea is a sparkling jewel as is the Library. Why do you think the Library is built on the Mediterranean Sea?
       Your answer may be:
       I believe that the Library is built on the Mediterranean Sea *because* Alexandria, Egypt, which was the original home of it, is on the same site.

   B. Using adjectives, describe an aspect of the Library of which you are aware.
       For example:
       The Library is digital.

Your sentence: _____

VI. Zanzibar said, "Pete, please bring some friends to help us introduce." Pete **Preposition** soon led a line of <u>prepositions</u> introducing topics. Singing a song, the group coming along included: of, to, in, at, about, over, above and on. Zanzibar explained that these powerful, little words are essential in sentence creation.

   A. In the sentences write an appropriate preposition:
       1) The Library is (**on**) the Mediterranean Sea. She looked (**at**) the sea often.
       2) The clock rang seven times (**in**) the morning and I awakened and went (**to**) the Library.

   B. Choose the best preposition for the following sentences or phrases from the choices shown after the sentences:
       1) The digital nature (**of**) the Library is helpful in communicating with people (**in**) the world. [of, on, in]
       2) Perhaps the digital aspect (**of**) the Library can help communicate all (**over**) the world. [from, of, over]

Your sentence: _____

VII. Connie **Conjunction**, always connecting asked, "Where is this Library built and where is it located? **Conjunctions connect two or more words, clauses or phrases; examples. are: for, and, not, but, or, yet** and **so**. Our purpose is to connect," she smiled **and** repeated with pride.

- It was built in Alexandria, Egypt *and* is located there.
- It is located on the Mediterranean Sea *but* not on the Red Sea.

    A. What words in the two sentences above are conjunctions?
    The words *and* and *but* in the sentences above are conjunctions.

    B. Which words in the following sentences are conjunctions? To answer underline the conjunctions in the sentences below: The single boys went to the dance as a group **but** they were hopeful of meeting girls **both** single **and** without a date. Regrettably, upon arrival, no girls **both** single **and** without a date were present **yet** some were expected to arrive later.

Your sentence: _____

VIII. Ike **Interjection** cawed, "We finished! The building is complete. Now we need to always be alert for any changes to keep it so. Interjections inject information into a story."

    A. Write sentences that may have been spoken at the time of the fire thousands of years ago using an Interjection.
    "Help!" The Library is burning! "Oh! The words are going up in flames!" squawked Ike, in horror.

    B. Write a sentence explaining **Why** you think that a toucan bird is the representative for interjections?
    Toucan birds are colorful and noisy; therefore, noticeable when they interrupt.

Your sentence: _____

    Ali, far in the future, analyzed—"Hmm, let me see."

Zanzibar was moving them out the door quickly.
Ali heard Zanzibar say:

Nouns to the fore!	*Name subject*
Verbs are at the door!	*Create Action/State of Being*
Adjectives modify nouns & pronouns.	*Describe*
Adverbs are modifying verbs & their equivalents.	*Describe*
"A little more detail, you say? Prepositional phrases lead the way.	
Prepositions be ready to join your object at the door.	**Detail**
Pronouns can replace you when you feel tired and need to snore.	*Replace*
Conjunctions connect us together.	*Connect*
Interjections interrupt and remind us forever of the sharp moments of clarity	*Inject*

When it was ever so simple to see

The beautiful words of The Library

***Zanzibar said,
"Now crew, go to the International Space Station, drink some espresso,
have a chat, then get some rest!"***

Questions on pages 22 - 25

Linda Smith Masi

<u>Time to dance to the beat!:</u>
<u>On your feet!</u>

Why We've Strived
<u>Zanzibar—Camel</u>

Responsible for reconstruction of old sentences and construction of new ones and his Zany Crew of Sentence Constructors:

<u>Noun-Nan Noun-giraffe</u> <u>Adverb-Anna Adverb-gazelle</u>
<u>Pronoun-Paul Pronoun-chameleon</u> <u>Preposition-Pete Preposition-zebra</u>
<u>Verb-Veronica Verb-monkey</u> <u>Conjunction-Connie</u>
  <u>Conjunction-chimpanzee</u>
<u>Adjective-Alfred Adjective-elephant</u> <u>Interjection-Ike Interjection</u>

<u>Ali-, Master of Zanzibar</u>
<u>far away in Outer Space</u>

to a rap beat

the accented words are in **bold**

<u>Why We've Strived</u>

"Let's keep it **alive—Everyone** come over **here** and **Jive!**
Verb pronoun(contraction), *verb, pronoun, adjective—Pronoun, verb,*
preposition, noun, conjunction, noun!

Words make us **thrive.**
Noun, verb, adverb, verb.

<u>They</u>   **bring**   us   to   our   **feet**   so
Pronoun,   verb,   pronoun,   prep.,   pronoun,   noun,   conj.

We   can   **dance**   and   keep the **beat**
Pronoun, conjunction, verb,   adjective, noun

Let's   **go**   sing   in   the   **street!**
Verb' pron. (contraction), *verb, verb, preposition, adjective, noun!*

<u>Hallelujah!!!!!!</u> For the moment, everything is **complete.** Together we've **strived**.
Interjection!!!!! Prep., adj., noun, pronoun, verb, adj. Adverb pron. 'verb.

Together we've **arrived!!!!!!**
Adverb, pron. 'verb(contraction), *verb!!!!!!!!*

Zanzibar and his Zany Crew of Sentence Constructors

The crew sang out, "Remind us again, Zanzibar!" "We've learned so many new things. Before we go to work, give us color clues to help us remember please." Zanzibar with a joyful roar replied: "To construct sentences what do we need?" Just look at this summary of our crew. It is really fun making sentences with you! Remember, most of the time we may be described like this:

1. Noun: Giraffe — *Names* the *Subject- what it's all about*

2. Pronoun: Gecko — *Replaces* the *Noun*

3. Verb: Monkey — *Expresses* the *Predicate- action* or *state of being*

4. Adjective: Elephant — *Describes Nouns*

5. Adverb: Gazelle — *Describes Verbs*

6. Conjunction: Chimpanzee — *Connects Words* or *Phrases*

7. Preposition: Zebra — *Introduces Words* or *Phrases*

8. Interjection: *Toucan* Bird — *Exclaims!* and *Interrupts!*

Resources

1. Webster's New Collegiate Dictionary, ©1981 by G. & C. Merriam Co.
Philippines Copyright 1981 by G. & C. Merriam Co.
Library of Congress Cataloging in Publication Data
Main entry under title:
Webster's new collegiate dictionary.
Editions for 1898-1948 have title: Webster's collegiate dictionary.
Includes index.

2. English language-Dictionaries
PE1628.W4M4 1981 423 80-25144
ISBN 0-87779-408-1
ISBN 0-87779-409-x (indexed)
ISBN 0-87779-410-3 (deluxe)
Webster's New Collegiate Dictionary principal copyright 1973
COLLEGIATE trademark Reg. U.S. Pat. Off.

3. clean, well-lighted sentences, © 2008 by Janis Bell
ISBN 978-0-393-06771-2
PE1441.B43 2008
429.2-dc22

W.W. Norton & Company, Inc.
500 Fifth Avenue, New York, N.Y. 10110
WWW.WWNORTON.COM

Please join us again soon

Zanzibar and his Zany Crew
are planning . . .

Anna Adverb quietly said, "This is too important for it to end." Zanzibar wisely said, "It is not we who will decide the end. We have the tools, we must keep going, I contend."

So, pick up your pen or use a computer to digit in the thoughts you wish to convey.
Try to write every day!

Please join us again soon
Zanzibar and his Zany Crew
are planning . . .

Exciting new adventures in English that await you!

Linda Smith Masi

The author's life with her husband and children at home in the USA, and later abroad in Europe and Asia has contributed to creating a unique perspective for this book. Also contributing to the viewpoint in the writing of this story is the influence of having lived near NASA in Houston, Texas with a family interested in the Space Program. Born in Dallas, Texas; Linda Smith Masi, the author, has an Honors degree from the University of Texas at Austin. She is a CPA, has training as an ISO 9000 Lead Auditor and is currently the president of Continuous Clear Communications (CCC), an entity providing editing and training in both oral and written English.

She served as the Chair of the International and the Health Care Committees of the Texas Society of CPAs in Houston. Mrs. Masi has written operational and financial manuals and implemented them by training the staff of international companies and hospitals. Her activity as a CPA also includes development of internal auditing programs with training-staff implementation. From 1983-1986 she created and operated an import wholesale distribution business of gift items wholesaling the products in the USA. Currently she is an English lecturer/ conversationalist in secondary schools, editor of scholarly documents and collaborator with teachers of English in Italy, where she lives with her husband. Her professional activity focuses on clear, efficient communications using English.